# Acupuncturist

VIRGINIA LOH-HAGAN

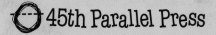
## 45th Parallel Press

Published in the United States of America by Cherry Lake Publishing
Ann Arbor, Michigan
www.cherrylakepublishing.com

Content Adviser: Brodie Burris, acupuncturist, owner of The Lotus Center, Ann Arbor, MI
Reading Adviser: Marla Conn, ReadAbility, Inc.
Book Design: Felicia Macheske

Photo Credits: © Chinaview / Shutterstock.com, cover, 1; © John Gomez / Shutterstock.com, 5; © Andrey_Popov / Shutterstock.com, 6; © Monkey Business Images / Shutterstock.com, 9; © stevecoleimages / iStock, 11; © Domenic Gareri / Shutterstock.com, 13; © leezsnow / iStock, 15; © kokouu / iStock, 16-17; © CHINE NOUVELLE/SIPA / Newscom, 19; © 4X-image / Thinkstock, 21; © Amoklv / Dreamstime.com, 23; © Elena Elisseeva / Shutterstock, 25; © bikec / Shutterstock, 27; © Trish233 / iStock, 28; © ARENA Creative / Shutterstock.com, cover and multiple interior pages; © oculo / Shutterstock.com, multiple interior pages; © Denniro / Shutterstock.com, multiple interior pages; © PhotoHouse / Shutterstock.com, multiple interior pages; © Miloje / Shutterstock.com, multiple interior pages

**45th Parallel Press** is an imprint of Cherry Lake Publishing.

Library of Congress Cataloging-in-Publication Data

Loh-Hagan, Virginia, author.
  Acupuncturist / Virginia Loh-Hagan.
     pages cm. — (Odd jobs)
  Summary: "From the interesting and intriguing to the weird and wonderful, Acupuncturist is HIGH interest combined with a LOW level of complexity to help struggling readers along. The carefully written, considerate text will hold readers' interest and allow for successful mastery, understanding, and enjoyment of reading about acupuncturists. Clear, full-color photographs with captions provide additional accessible information. A table of contents, glossary with simplified pronunciations, and index all enhance achievement and comprehension."— Provided by publisher.
  Includes bibliographical references and index.
  ISBN 978-1-63470-030-6 (hardcover) — ISBN 978-1-63470-057-3 (pbk.) — ISBN 978-1-63470-084-9 (pdf) — ISBN 978-1-63470-111-2 (ebook)
1. Acupuncturists—Juvenile literature. 2. Acupuncture—Vocational guidance—Juvenile literature.
3. Alternative medicine—Juvenile literature. I. Title.

RM184.L63 2016
615.8'92—dc23
                           2015008260

Cherry Lake Publishing would like to acknowledge the work of The Partnership for 21st Century Skills. Please visit *www.p21.org* for more information.

Printed in the United States of America
Corporate Graphics Inc.

# Contents

# CHAPTER 1

# Relieving Pain

What is Eastern medicine? What is acupuncture? What is alternative medicine? Why use acupuncture?

David Fridovich was in charge of the U.S. Special Forces. He was a soldier. He served on many secret missions. He jumped from planes. He hurt his back. He hurt his leg. He said he couldn't eat or sleep. He was in pain. So Fridovich took pain drugs. He got hooked. He couldn't stop taking them.

He tried **acupuncture**. Acupuncture relieves pain. It's Eastern medicine. It's from China. China is in the Far East. Acupuncturists put needles in specific points of the body.

Fridovich said, "Western medicine doesn't have all the answers." Some people don't want drugs. They don't want operations. Acupuncture is an option.

_Acupuncture comes from two Latin words. Acus means "needle." Punctura means "to puncture."_

Dr. Rochelle Wasserman is a military doctor. She treats soldiers at the Warrior Care Clinic. She's also an acupuncturist. She got acupuncture. She felt better. So she gives it to soldiers. She likes **alternative** medicine. Alternative means different.

*Military doctors treat soldiers on battlefields. Air Force doctors developed "battlefield acupuncture." They give acupuncture for operations.*

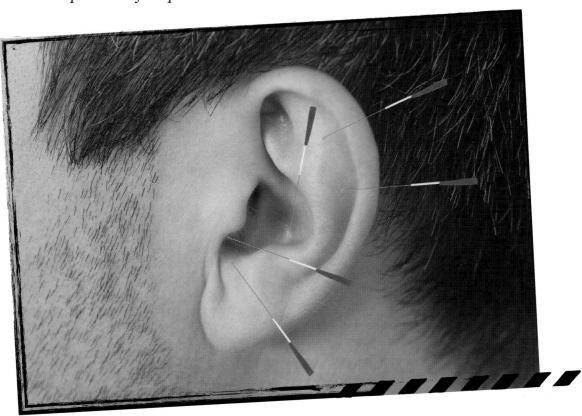

# WHEN ODD IS TOO ODD!

Katy Perry is a pop singer. She tweeted about eating "the best sushi." Sushi is a special fish dish from Japan. The fish she ate had been treated with acupuncture. Chef Antonio Park prepared the fish. Park developed this technique of fish acupuncture. It's known as *kaimin katsugyo*. This means "live fish sleeping soundly." Fishermen insert needles into the fish. This relieves fish from the pain of death. It makes the fish taste better. The acupuncture keeps fish alive but sleepy. This is a kinder way to die. It also keeps the fish fresh. Park says, "Freshness is about the search for purity in the taste of the fish. You want to taste the maximum flavor from the fish."

Rick Remalia is one of her **patients**. A patient needs a doctor. He was hurt in battle. He hurt his shoulder. He broke his back. He broke his hip. He walks with a cane. He has a brain injury. He's always in pain.

Wasserman put tiny needles in his ears. This was the first treatment that worked. Rick's headaches are gone. He takes fewer drugs.

Doctors use acupuncture to relieve **physical** pain. Physical means the body. They also use it to relieve **mental** pain. Mental means the mind.

Dr. Robert L. Koffman is a navy **psychiatrist**. A psychiatrist treats mental health. He's also an acupuncturist. Many soldiers get **depressed**, or very sad. They get stressed. They get scared.

Koffman helps soldiers' mental health. War hurts people's bodies. It hurts people's minds. Acupuncture helps them. They feel better.

*Soldiers in battle have a hard time sleeping.*
*They have a hard time relaxing. Acupuncture helps them.*

# CHAPTER 2

# Relieving Injuries

Why do sports players need acupuncturists?
How do acupuncturists help athletes?

Acupuncture relieves people's illnesses. It helps people heal.

Football players get injured a lot. Some football teams hire acupuncturists. They travel with the team. Dr. Evan Mladenoff was the first team acupuncturist.

Aaron Rodgers is a football player. He hurt his leg. He used acupuncture. It helped his pain and

**inflammation**. Inflammation means red and swollen. It slows healing. Rodgers needs healthy legs. Acupuncture is part of his daily treatment.

*Brain scientists found that putting needles into muscles helps repair the tissue.*

## Spotlight Biography
# HARO OGAWA

Haro Ogawa is the acupuncturist for the San Francisco Giants. He's worked for other sports teams. He was born in Japan. He had back pain. He spent time in a wheelchair. An acupuncturist helped him. This inspired him to become an acupuncturist. He said, "I wanted to help people in pain." Baseball players get hurt. Ogawa helps them so they can play. He travels with the team. He works 81 home games and 81 road games. He said, "The thing that makes me the happiest is when a player tells me, 'Thank you very much' or 'You are the best!' It means a great deal to earn trust from the ballplayers and the team as a whole." Ogawa tried other jobs. He finished law school in Japan. He worked in real estate. But he finds acupuncture more rewarding. He said, "It's tough. But it's fun."

Captain Munnerlyn plays football. He was training. He injured his leg. He visited an acupuncturist. It got him back on the field in a week.

Other athletes get acupuncture. Jason Giambi played baseball. He got acupuncture. He said it's helped him.

Jamie Starkey was his baseball team's acupuncturist. She said, "I can go in and actually release some of the muscles that may be tight, and that would actually prevent injury down the road."

Dwyane Wade plays basketball. He hurt his knee. He said, "You just try to find a way to feel a little better." He's scared of needles. But acupuncture helped him.

_Acupuncture treats body pain. It also treats nausea, headaches, anxiety, and insomnia._

# CHAPTER 3

# Handling Needles

**What is the connection between acupuncture and energy? What is qi? How do acupuncturists learn about their patients? Why do acupuncturists use needles?**

Acupuncturists see the body as an energy field. Acupuncture balances that energy. It **stimulates** the body. Stimulate means to excite.

**Qi**, or chi, is a person's life force. It flows through the body. It flows through 12 organs. It flows through 12

**meridians**. Meridians are points in the body. The points are connected.

Acupuncturists ask questions. They check the person's **pulse**, or heartbeat. They check the person's tongue. They check the person's skin. They smell the person's body. They ask where the pain is. Pain indicates blocked qi.

*Everyone has different needs. Acupuncturists choose the best treatment.*

*Some people don't feel the needles. Some feel a twitch or tingling.*

Acupuncturists use needles to move qi. Needles come in many types and sizes. There's a different needle for each body part and problem.

The person lies on a padded table. Acupuncturists clean the area. They put needles into meridians. They tap, twirl, or jiggle each needle. They insert some needles deeper than others.

After the needles are inserted, the person rests. Some people sleep. Sessions last 15 to 60 minutes. At the end, acupuncturists take out the needles.

Sometimes, acupuncturists heat the needles. Sometimes, they burn herbs. It gives off smoke and a nice smell. Sometimes, they send electricity through the needles. Sometimes, they use a cold laser or a low light. This stimulates points that needles can't reach.

## Advice from the Field
# RICHARD MANDELL

Richard Mandell is an acupuncturist. He taught at the New England School of Acupuncture. He's the founder and executive director of The PanAfrican Acupuncture Project. He trains people in Africa. He teaches them how to use acupuncture. He helps people with sicknesses. He said, "I have come to believe that people need connection more than anything else. We, acupuncturists, use needles as a starting point. But it is our relationship with patients—the conversations, the gentle touch—that is most important." He encourages people to be helpful. He thinks acupuncturists build and move good energy by connecting with people.

To be acupuncturists, people have to study. They go to college. They go to acupuncture school. They pass tests. They work with acupuncturists. They get a **license**. A license shows they have proper training.

Acupuncturists must follow rules. They must be prepared. They handle needles correctly. They use clean needles. They throw away used needles.

Poorly trained acupuncturists have hurt people. They have hurt organs. Dirty needles cause infections. They spread sicknesses.

*Acupuncturists want to help people. They need to train and study.*

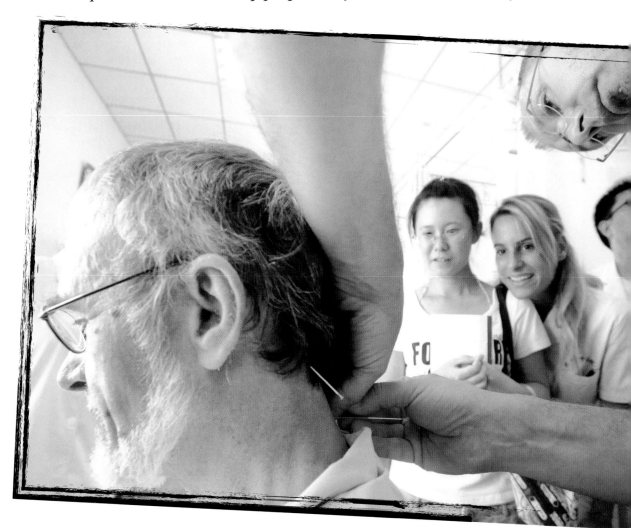

# CHAPTER 4

# History and Challenges

What is the history of acupuncture? Who is Otzi? How did acupuncture become popular in the United States? What is a challenge acupuncturists face?

Acupuncture is old. No one knows how it started. Most people think it started in China. They think it started 3,000-4,000 years ago.

The earliest acupuncture needles are from the Stone Age. People used sharp stones called **bian**. Needles improved over time. They were made from bone, bamboo, bronze, iron, gold, and silver. Today's needles are stainless steel.

Otzi the Iceman is a 5,000-year-old mummy. He was found in Europe. He had many **tattoos**. Tattoos are permanent drawings on the skin. Otzi's tattoos were acupuncture points. This means acupuncture is very old. It also means it was used outside of China.

---

*Acupuncture spread from China along trade routes.*

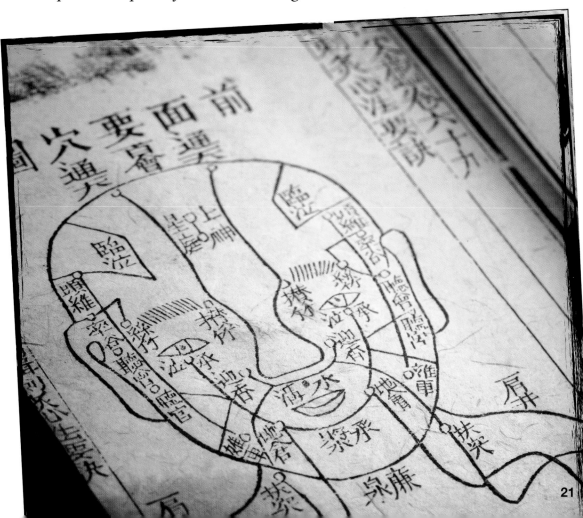

## Acupuncturist
# KNOW THE LINGO!

**Acupoints:** more than 360 specific acupuncture points on the body, located on meridians

**Acupressure:** acupuncture without needles, applying pressure instead of needles

**Deficiency:** too little energy

**Excess:** too much energy

**Jing:** essence; energy inherited from parents

**Shen:** spirit

**Stagnation:** blocked energy that doesn't flow freely

**Taiji:** interplay between yin and yang; all movement and change

**TCM (traditional Chinese medicine):** medical system including acupuncture, herbal therapy, bodywork, breath work, moxibustion, and exercise

**Vessels:** containers of energy in the body

**Wei:** defense energy connected to the immune system

**Yang:** hot, active, restless, transforming energy

**Yin:** cooling, calming, relaxing, conserving energy

**Ying:** nutritional energy

**Zhong:** energy supplemented through breath; controls movement of blood especially to the hands and feet

In the 1970s, acupuncture became popular in the United States. This is when President Nixon visited China. Americans became interested in Chinese things.

James Reston was a news reporter. He traveled with President Nixon. He got sick in China. He had to get an operation. He was in pain. He got acupuncture. He felt better. He was impressed.

Reston wrote about it. He wrote that the acupuncturist "inserted three long, thin needles into the outer part of my right elbow and below my knees." Twenty minutes later, Reston felt relaxed. His article made people interested in acupuncture.

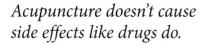

*Acupuncture doesn't cause side effects like drugs do.*

Over the years, acupuncturists have faced challenges. Not everyone believes in acupuncture.

Dr. Harriet Hall is a military doctor. She thinks acupuncture is like a fake pill. It just makes people believe they're better. She said, "The idea that putting needles in somebody's ear is going to substitute for things like **morphine** is just ridiculous." Morphine is a drug for pain.

Acupuncturists must prove they're helping people. They spend more time with their patients. They take time to diagnose. They find the causes of problems. They study how the body works. They say acupuncture releases natural painkillers.

*Acupuncture is the most trusted type of alternative medicine.*

# CHAPTER 5

# Not Just for People!

How do acupuncturists help animals?
Who is Bubba?

Acupuncturists help animals, too. **Vets**, or veterinarians, are animal doctors.

Edurne Cornejo is a veterinary acupuncturist. Her patient is an owl. The owl is 10 inches (25 centimeters) tall. It hurt its back. It flew into a stovepipe. The owl was sent to a rescue park.

Cornejo puts needles into the owl's legs. The

needles help the owl. The owl has had at least 10 sessions.

Cornejo said, "When he first came, he couldn't stand up. Then he started taking little steps. Now he is flying again."

Some vets use acupuncture to treat pet problems.

Bubba is a Komodo dragon. He is over 20 years old. He lives at the San Antonio Zoo. He has bone disease in both knees. He has a hard time moving.

Rob Coke is a vet at the zoo. He gives Bubba acupuncture. Bubba gets weekly treatment. At first, Bubba fought acupuncture. Five people had to hold Bubba. Bubba has relaxed. Coke sees improvement.

Acupuncture is an odd job. But it improves the lives of people and animals.

*Many doctors use Eastern and Western medicine to treat patients.*

# THAT HAPPENED?!?

Xu Long is from China. He said, "The only time I ever had acupuncture was while in the army. I recall I had an ongoing stomach ache at the time, which hurt for two days and two nights. The army doctor offered to perform acupuncture on me and it worked. The pain stopped immediately." This was in 1974. For the next 40 years, he complained of chest and back pains. The doctor told him it was old age. Doctors finally decided to x-ray him. They found an acupuncture needle. It was stuck in his stomach for 40 years. He had surgery to remove it. The doctor said, "The needle, which was stuck in his intestines, had turned black and was very thick."

# DID YOU KNOW?

- Mohanathas Sivanayagam set a record. He stuck 2,100 acupuncture needles into his head. Each needle was inserted 0.6 inches (1.5 cm) deep. He didn't want the needles to fall out. He learned from an acupuncturist. He took breaks. He didn't want to cramp his hands. When he moved his jaw, he felt the needles move. He couldn't lie down. It took him 48 hours. He drank 10 large coffees to stay awake. He said, "When it comes to needles, people are scared." He wanted people to not be scared of acupuncture.

- Fanny Pachon fights for animal rights. She's against bullfighting. She thinks it's cruel. The bulls are stuck with spears like needles. David Hernandez is an acupuncturist. He put about 2,500 needles in her back. She wanted to show bullfighters how the bulls feel.

- Lisa Ripi is a traveling acupuncturist. She works for the National Football League. She treats about 40 players on five teams. She's not a football fan. But she loves her football players. She said, "They come first. Before anything. Before me." She can tell a player's position by where they have pain.

- Acupuncturists study people's tongues. Teeth marks on one part of the tongue might mean heart problems. Teeth marks on another part of the tongue might mean liver problems.

- Mao Zedong, the leader of China for many years, promoted acupuncture in public. But he did not believe in it. He also didn't use it.

- There are about 360 acupoints on the 12 major meridians. Acupuncturists use about 100 of those points on a daily basis.

- An average dog needs 15 to 20 needles. The needles are about 0.25 to 0.5 inches (0.6 to 1.3 cm) deep. They are left in for 20 minutes. Horses need around 30 needles. Some needles are 3 to 4 inches (7.6 to 10 cm) long.

# CONSIDER THIS!

**TAKE A POSITION!** Acupuncture heals some types of pain. But it doesn't heal other types of pain. Many Western doctors and scientists disagree about the value of acupuncture. Do you think people should consider acupuncture as part of their medical treatment plan?

**SAY WHAT?** Dr. Rochelle Wasserman said, "I actually prefer the term *integrative medicine*. We use anything that might be helpful to our soldiers in addition to what most would consider traditional or conventional standard medicines." Explain this quotation. Explain the different health options people have today.

**THINK ABOUT IT!** Acupuncture has become popular in the United States. It came from China. What other things came from China? What type of relationship does the United States have with China?

**SEE A DIFFERENT SIDE!** Some people disagree with the use of alternative medicine. They don't think acupuncture is scientific. Learn more about their position. Do you agree or disagree with their perspective?

---

## LEARN MORE

### PRIMARY SOURCES

"Escape Fire: The Fight to Rescue American Healthcare," a documentary that supports alternative medicine like acupuncture: www.escapefiremovie.com/trailer

Tattoo Odyssey, a documentary (Smithsonian Channel, 2010).

Oprah's First Acupuncture Session: www.oprah.com/oprahshow/Watch-Oprahs-First-Acupuncture-Session-Video

### SECONDARY SOURCES

Cotterell, Arthur. *Ancient China*. New York: DK Publishing, 2005.

Lindsay, Judy. *The Story of Medicine: From Acupuncture to X-Rays*. New York: Oxford University Press, 2003.

Parker, Steve. *Medicine*. London; New York: Dorling Kindersley, 2000.

### WEB SITES

American Academy of Medical Acupuncture: www.medicalacupuncture.org

American Association of Acupuncture and Oriental Medicine: www.aaaomonline.org/

National Certification Commission for Acupuncture and Oriental Medicine: www.nccaom.org

## GLOSSARY

**acupuncture** (AK-yoo-pungk-chur) Eastern medicine in which needles are inserted in specific points of the body

**alternative** (awl-TUR-nuh-tiv) different option

**bian** (BEE-yin) pointy stone used to heal

**depressed** (dih-PREST) deeply unhappy

**inflammation** (in-fluh-MAY-shuhn) when body parts become red and swollen

**license** (LYE-suhns) permission granted to perform duties; ensures proper training

**mental** (MEN-tuhl) of the mind

**meridians** (muh-RID-ee-uhnz) special points in the body

**morphine** (mor-FEEN) a drug used for pain

**patients** (PAY-shuhnts) people who are sick and need a doctor

**physical** (FIZ-ih-kuhl) of the body

**psychiatrist** (sye-KYE-uh-trist) doctor of mental health

**pulse** (PUHLS) heartbeat

**qi** (KEE) also called chi; life force that flows through the body

**stimulates** (STIM-yuh-lates) excites

**tattoos** (tah-TOOZ) permanent drawings on the skin

**vets** (VETS) short for veterinarians; animal doctors

## INDEX

## ABOUT THE AUTHOR

Dr. Virginia Loh-Hagan is an author, university professor, former classroom teacher, and curriculum designer. She likes all things Chinese, even acupuncture. But she likes dim sum food more. She lives in San Diego with her very tall husband and very naughty dogs. To learn more about her, visit www.virginialoh.com.